CONTENTS

C000121448

INTRODUCTION

Moated sites, where a house and its associated buildings were protected by a wide ditch filled with water, seem to have been popular from around 1200 to around 1325. Scholars are not agreed as to whether they were primarily defensive, or chosen as an effective means of drainage, or merely served as status symbols. No doubt they could serve a number of purposes. They were not impregnable against concerted attack, but would have deterred the depredations of raiders and thieves in the unsettled times of the 13th and early 14th centuries.

Moats are normally associated with high-status buildings, such as manor houses or monastic granges, but can also be found around humbler establishments, especially those remote from areas of settlement.

Few remain in use, though some can be traced in the landscape, while others are only known from map and other documentary evidence.

In 1969 the late Dennis Turner published a 'Provisional list of moated sites in N.E. Surrey',[1] which included three sites in Merton, two in Mitcham and one in Morden:

Merton   WEST BARNES (TQ 226685). 19th-century map evidence suggests that this farm was once moated. It was originally a grange of Merton Priory. Site now covered by school buildings.

             MERTON PLACE (TQ 261700). Illustrations and descriptions of this one-time home of Lord Nelson show that it was partially moated. Whether the moat was the remains of a genuine medieval site or whether it was part of a gardening extravaganza is not clear.

             S.W. of ST MARY'S CHURCH (TQ 250694). 19th-century map evidence suggests that there was possibly once a moated site here.

Mitcham   RAVENSBURY (TQ 265681). Water channels enclosing a rectangular area may merely be connected with water mills. A large pond, possibly a medieval fish-pond, immediately to the east, has now been filled in and built over.

             THE CANONS (TQ 279683). The pond to the east of the house could be the remains of a moat. The site is that of a medieval manor.

Morden   MORDEN HALL (TQ 260687). A complex enclosure probably considerably altered when the present house was built in 1770.

Two sites within Wimbledon were also included, but they lie outside the scope of Merton Historical Society and within the remit of the Wimbledon Society, and so will not be considered further in this study:

Wimbledon OLD RECTORY (TQ 244715). The writer recalls reading a statement to the effect that the Old Rectory was once moated but cannot now trace the reference. Corroborative evidence is needed.

BURLINGTON ROAD (TQ 240717). Moat-like ditches marked on the Tithe Award Map are probably merely outflows connected with the nearby lakes.

Dennis Turner followed this in 1977 with 'Moated Sites in Surrey: a provisional List',[2] which split the sites between 'Certain and Probable Sites' and 'Doubtful Sites'. The first category included:

Merton MERTON PLACE (TQ 260700)

WEST BARNES (TQ 226685) – Map evidence only

Morden MORDEN HALL (TQ 259686)

while the doubtful sites included:

Merton NEAR RECTORY (TQ 250694)

Mitcham THE CANNONS [*sic*] (TQ 279683)

MITCHAM HALL (TQ 274683)

RAVENSBURY (TQ 266681)

In some cases there is a slight disparity between the grid reference on each list, as the feature is larger than a single cell. The spelling of Canons in the second list is almost certainly a typographical error introduced at the editorial stage. Dennis was a long-time resident of Merton and active within Merton Historical Society for many years, and knew the area well.

Since this list was published, Eric Montague has put forward another possible site, at Colliers Wood House, and I would like to consider yet another, Mitcham Grove.

This study examines the evidence currently available for each of the sites within the present London Borough of Merton, except for the two Wimbledon sites.

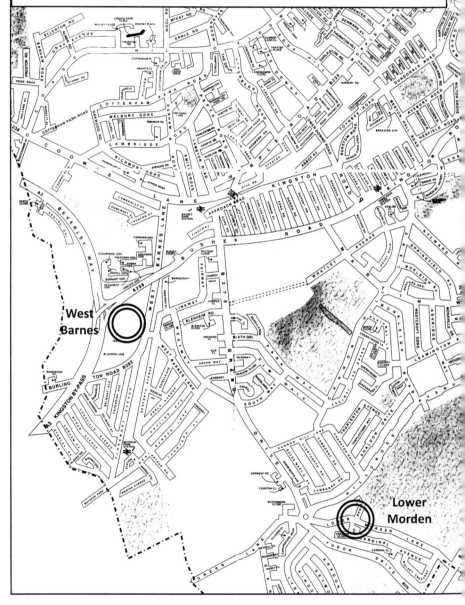

Detail from a modern street map, showing the sites discussed in this book. Reproduced by permission of Merton Design Unit, London Borough of Merton

West Barnes

Lower Morden

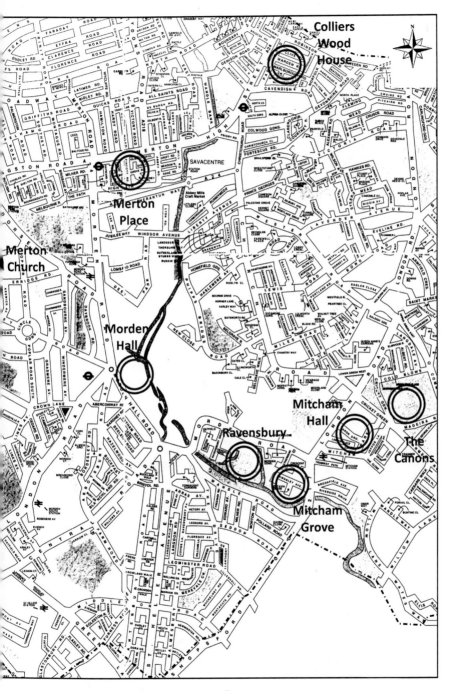

Colliers
Wood
House

Merton
Place

Merton
Church

Morden
Hall

Ravensbury

Mitcham
Hall

The
Canons

Mitcham
Grove

MERTON PLACE

The earliest account of the origins of the house is in an indenture of lease and release dated 22 June 1792, in which Sir Richard Hotham bargained and sold to Charles Greaves, William Hodgson, James Newton and John Leach

> all that capital messuage heretofore built and erected by Henry Pratt Esq. situate in the parishes of Merton and Wimbledon, or one of them, which with the lands hereinafter mentioned were formerly called Moat House Farm, but several alterations and additions having been lately made to the said capital messuage by the said Sir Richard Hotham and the same having been greatly enlarged and improved the said capital messuage for some time past hath been and now is known by the name of and called Merton Place ... [3]

Only the house site – some 1½ acres – was within Merton parish, the remaining lands being within Wimbledon parish, north of the road.

Pratt had bought the land in June 1748,[4] and insured the property with the Sun Insurance Company in August 1753.[5] The site (circled) had been shown on John Rocque's *Map of Ten Miles around London* of 1741–5, and the curving leat from the western course of the Wandle, feeding a pond and the moat that gave the site its name, is clearly shown.

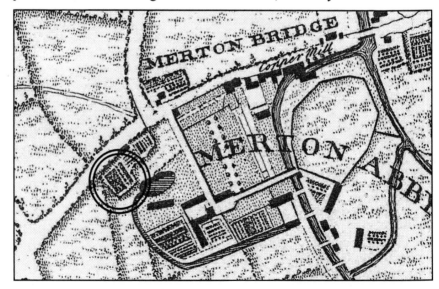

Pratt's son sold the property to Hotham in 1764,[6] and it seems certain that the black rectangle (circled) depicted on Rocque's *Map of Surrey* from 1768 represents the moat surrounding the house.

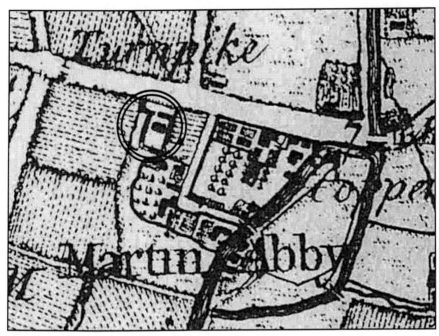

Sir William and Lady Hamilton recommended this site to Nelson for his new home, and he completed the purchase in October 1801,[7] despite his surveyor's adverse comments:

> There are so many insurmountable objections as a Residence, that I am astonished anyone can think of it as nearly compleat for any family ... [8]

One of his comments related to the moat that had given its name to the original house, which was

> circumscribed by a dirty black looking canal, or rather a broad ditch, which keeps the whole place damp.

However, Emma Hamilton treated the 'ditch' as a feature rather than a liability, calling it 'The Nile', after Nelson's victory in Aboukir Bay, and it takes pride of place in contemporary engravings, such as those reproduced on the front cover and overleaf.[9]

The 'Canal' is shown on this extract from the plan accompanying the sales particulars of 1823, when the site of the house was auctioned.[10]

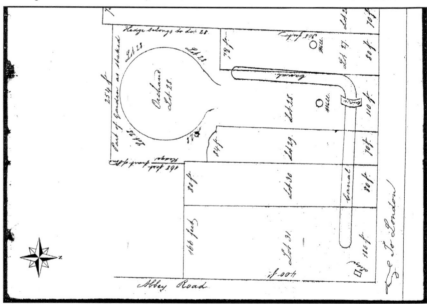

The plan gives the measurements of each of the 31 lots described in the sales particulars as 'adequate for detached villas', no.28 having the note

'Upon this Lot the Mansion recently stood'. Only two arms of the moat had survived, and these were soon to disappear.

But what was the origin of this moat, which clearly predated Pratt's house? Contemporary maps show that the house was very close to the precinct wall of Merton priory, called 'Merton Abby' or 'Martin Abby' on Rocque's maps. A document of 1538 records that in April 1533 the prior and convent had leased to John Hyller for 21 years

> a certain parcel of the demesne of Merton pertaining to the Grange there situate outside the gates of the said late priory [detailed schedule of fields] with all buildings and curtilages pertaining to the same Grange, with a certain house with garden which the farmer inhabits. Except that the prior and convent reserves to itself and its successors the dovehouse, ponds, fisheries, woods and underwood, trees and all firewood, and all other commodities, liberties and franchises to them pertaining, with free ingress and egress through the whole of the said premises, and of holding their Court and View of frank-pledge within the Grange whenever and as often as they please ... And the same John is to repair and maintain all ditches and fences of the said Grange with its appurtenances.[11]

Thus the Grange was immediately outside the gate, and granges were often moated.[12] But Merton Place could not have been located within the moated site of the former Grange outside the gates of Merton priory, as Nelson had bought Merton Place in October 1801, and it was not until November 1802 that he purchased the adjoining 114-acre Merton Grange estate.[13] In his will Nelson bequeathed to Emma Hamilton

> my capital messuage at Merton, in the county of Surry, and the out-houses, offices, gardens and pleasure grounds belonging thereto, and such parts of my grounds, farms, lands, tenements and hereditaments, in the several parishes of Merton, Wimbledon, and Mitcham, or any of them, as, together with, and including the site of the said messuage, out-houses, offices, gardens, pleasure grounds, shrubbery, canal, and mote, shall not exceed seventy-acres, as shall be selected by the said Emma, lady Hamilton, within six months after my decease.[14]

In addition to the 20 acres of the house and pleasure grounds, Emma selected the lawns and shrubberies within Wimbledon, and the following properties within Merton (measured in acres, roods and perches)

Farmery	1.0.14
Roadway	0.1.34
Barn field	6.0.30
Middle field	6.3.25
Sheephouse field	6.2.33

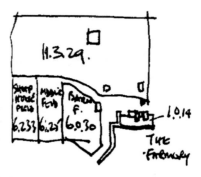

and these are depicted on the plan accompanying the deed recording her selection,[13] as shown in this sketch by the late John Wallace.

They can be identified as the 18 acres of plots 221–222 of the Merton tithe apportionment of 1844, named as 'Morden Six Acres' and 'Sheep House and Middle Field'.[15] (The superimposed outline marks the probable extent of the priory's Grange estate to the west and the precinct to the east.) 'One close called Shepshowse Close and Mychelle Close' is listed in the lease of the Grange to Hyller immediately before the farmer's house,[16] which probably indicates that the Farmery purchased by Nelson with the

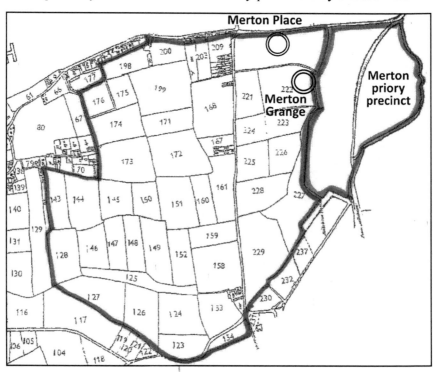

rest of the Merton Grange estate stood on the site of the 16th-century house. An extra-illustrated edition of Manning & Bray's *History and Antiquities of Surrey* in the British Library contains a drawing labelled 'A sketch of Merton Abbey Farm before it was pulled down for Lord Nelson's mansion. It was the birthplace of my father, Mr John Berryman, Free School master, Chertsey. Oct 1798 in going the annual rounds of visiting my relatives.'[17] Here is a copy sketched by John Wallace.

We have seen that Nelson did not pull down the house at Merton Place, though he greatly extended it. But a former tenant of Merton Grange before Nelson's purchase, occupying the 'house with barns, stables etc in Merton', was Thomas Berriman,[18] whose son John was baptised 28 October 1736.[19] There seems no doubt that Nelson's Farmery had replaced an earlier building on the site of the house belonging to Merton Grange, to the south of the site of Merton Place, and that this was the building depicted on Rocque's maps within the curve of the leat feeding the pond and the Merton Place moat. Had the leat served as a moat surrounding the domestic buildings of the priory's Grange, with the moat at Merton Place forming a secondary enclosure for ancillary buildings – a common feature within monastic moated granges?[20]

Hyller continued to occupy the Grange after the Dissolution in 1538, and in July 1553 the estate was granted by Letters Patent to John, earl of Warwick and Sir Henry Sidney,[21] and in May 1564 to Sir Henry Sidney alone, by which time Hyller had been replaced by William Tirrell.[22] Sidney sold 150 acres to Richard Garth, who had purchased the adjoining manor of Morden.[23] Some time between 1629 and 1651 the rest of the estate came into the hands of Rowland Wilson, who had purchased the former priory precinct in 1625.[24]

The precinct had been leased separately from the Grange, and the lessee for nearly 50 years was the queen's 'cofferer' or household treasurer, Sir Gregory Lovell. Following Lovell's death in 1597 an efficient county surveyor discovered that he had occupied some insignificant properties adjoining the precinct, for which no rent had been charged. His widow, Dorothy, was granted two 30-year leases for these extra properties, paying an additional 20 shillings in annual rent. One of these properties was described as

> all that parcel of land containing by estimation one rood of land enclosed with mote and hedges and one old dovehouse built and erected from of old upon the same parcel of land, lying and being in the parish of Merton aforesaid and abutting against the north upon the royal way leading from Merton aforesaid towards Tooting [25]

Thus we have an ancient moated site on a small plot immediately to the south of the High Street on the periphery of the priory precinct. This was presumably the dovehouse reserved by the priory when the Grange had been leased to Hyller in 1533.

Surprisingly, the surviving copy of the 1597 lease has a note to the appropriate government officials explaining the origin of the dovehouse:

> Yt seemeth by Auncient Surveye that the said parcel of grounde was inclosed owt of the waist on purpose to build the said dovehouse thereuppon for the provision of the said late Monastery and a mote cast aboute the said dovehouse within the said inclosed grounde for the saffe keeping of the doves.

The moated dovehouse remained part of the precinct estate until 1612, by which time the precinct had been purchased from the Crown. In 1601 Nicholas and Elizabeth Zouche had received licence to alienate to Charles earl of Nottingham and his wife Katherine

> the site of the former priory of Merton alias Marten alias Marton, and 1 messuage, 4 barns, 4 dovecotes, 4 gardens, 4 orchards, 100 acres land, 180 meadow, 80 pasture, 6 wood and 6 heath and furze, and 10s rents in Merton, Mitcham, Streatham and Long Ditton in county of Surrey. [26]

The Nottinghams sold to John Spylman in 1605, [27] who, with his wife, Elizabeth, and Anthony and Susan Ingram, sold to Thomas Cornwall in 1606. [28] Cornwall proceeded to break up the estate, [29] and the precinct was sold in 1610 to Thomas Marbury.[30] But in 1613, when Marbury sold to trustees of Sir Francis Clarke, the grant excluded 'a certain messuage and tenement formerly called le Duble Dovehouse belonging to the said late priory'.[31] This property had been sold the previous year to John Listnye, when it was described as

> all that messuage or tenement formerly a dovehouse enclosed with a ditch [*inclusis cum fodeum*] situate outside the walls of the late house of the dissolved priory of Merton alias Marton in the county of Surrey; and one piece of land containing one acre; and also the aforesaid ditch [*fodeum*] or *la moat* and scouring and soil of the same; and all shops [*shopas*], cellars, solars, barns, stables built thereon with orchards, gardens, easements and appurtenances pertaining to the messuage.[32]

It would seem that additional land, probably further encroachment upon roadside waste, had been added, bringing the property up to the 1½ acres recorded at the time of Nelson's purchase of Merton Place.

A similar description appeared in 1621 when Henry Carpenter received pardon for purchasing from Listnye in October 1612

> all that messuage or tenement formerly with the Great Dovehouse enclosed with ditches and walls being outside the walls of the late house of the dissolved priory of Merton alias Marten in the county of Surrey; and one parcel of land containing by estimation one acre; and land and soil of the same Dovehouse or house messuage aforesaid.[33]

A similar pardon was granted to Rowland Wilson in 1632 for acquiring from Henry Carpenter's brother Gregory and Gregory's youngest son William Carpenter

> all that messuage or tenement called by the name of the Double Dove House and all messuages, lands, tenements, meadows, orchards, buildings, stables, gardens, orchards, land, ... pertaining, and all hereditaments belonging to the same messuage or tenement situate, lying and being in Merton in the county of Surrey in the tenure of the said Gregory and his heirs.[34]

In 1635 a very belated pardon was granted to William Carpenter for receiving the property from his father in November 1624.[35] The Carpenters also owned West Barnes in Merton, to which we shall turn in the next section.

Wilson now owned the Precinct, the Grange and the Double Dovehouse, and all passed to his grandchildren, the eldest of whom was Ellis Crisp. Ellis had sold the site of Moat House Farm (the later Merton Place) in 1699 to William Hammond, whose grandson in turn sold it to Pratt in 1746. There seems little doubt that Moat House Farm was built on the site of the former moated dovehouse.

It may be pertinent that when the house was offered for sale in 1801 it contained 'a very extensive Servants Hall with a Strong Stone Closet and capital Iron Door',[36] and this is shown on Thomas Chawner's *Plan of the Entrance Story of Lord Nelson's House in Merton* of January 1805, reproduced below.[37]

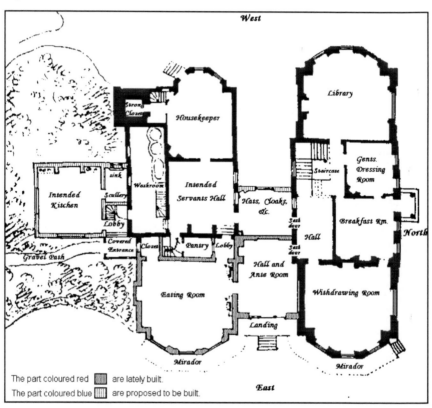

Could this stone closet have utilised part of the original dovehouse?

WEST BARNES

Merton priory had another large estate occupying the western section of the parish of Merton, and the name 'Westbarnys' appears in manorial court rolls from 1505.[38] A lease of 1536 is copied into Ministers Accounts for 1538 following the dissolution of the priory.[39] The property covered a total of 579 acres,[40] as outlined on this copy of the 1844 tithe map for Merton. (Only two sections of the estate were liable for tithes, so the remainder was left blank on the map with no plot numbers assigned.)

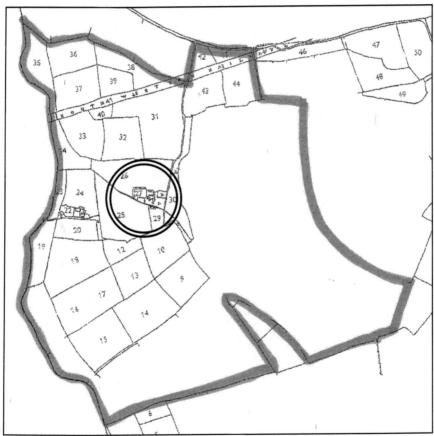

The estate was granted to Sir John Gresham in 1545,[41] and between 1567 and 1598 most was sold to his tenant, John Carpenter,[42] though one section, the later Blagdon Farm, was sold to Thomas Randall in February 1573/4.[43] The estate passed from John Carpenter's son Gregory, whom we have met above regarding the Double Dovehouse, to his son Robert, who divided the estate among his sons, the western section, including the old farmhouse (below),[44] going to his eldest, another John, while the eastern section was settled on his four younger sons. A further division had occurred by 1737 to create the farm known as Blue House Farm.

In 1811 John Middleton, owner of the eastern section of West Barnes, wrote to Surrey historian William Bray about some possibly Roman bricks 'dug out of the ruins of an ancient arch that had crossed a small rivulet or common sewer at West Barns in Merton, in the land of C. F. Bond Esq. about a hundred yards on the East side of a very old farm house, moated round, which formerly belonged to the Abbat and Monks of Merton'.[45] Middleton's nephew, Edward Rayne, whose name was appropriated for the station and development at Raynes Park, referred to the western farm as 'Moat Farm' in family correspondence in 1837,[46] and the Merton tithe apportionment of 1844 gives the name 'Moat Meadow' to plot 25, south of the farmhouse in plot 27. This meadow lay on the southern bank of the Pyl Brook which flows to its confluence with the Beverley Brook at the western edge of the estate. Remnants of the moat survived into the 20th century, and are shown on Ordnance Survey maps of 1913, reproduced below, and 1935. The site is now covered by the 1985-built gymnasium of Raynes Park High School.[47]

There seems little doubt that this was a medieval moated site, though whether the estate should be classed as a medieval grange, rather than a Tudor farm, is open to debate. Manorial court rolls reveal that all but three acres of the tenant lands in the former open fields had come into the hands of the priory by the end of the 15th century, enabling the creation of the large farms.

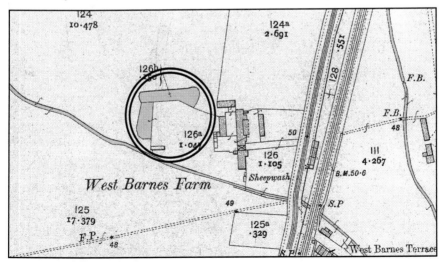

SOUTH-WEST OF ST MARY'S CHURCH, MERTON

A rectangular pond with rounded ends, in a field to the south-west of the ancient parish church of Merton, was shown on Ordnance Survey maps until 1913, though the extract below is from the map of 1894–6. It is within the grounds of the Vicarage (not Rectory as in Dennis Turner's second list), but the garden boundary has clearly been extended to include the pond, indicating that it already existed when the garden was established.

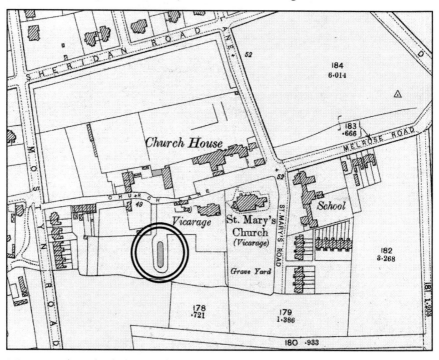

Merton priory had appropriated the rectorial tithes of the parish early in its history, perhaps even from its foundation in 1114, and certainly before 1340 when a document in the priory cartulary records Merton among 16 churches and chapels 'that the Prior and Convent possessed and held to their own proper use ... (with their tithes and appurtenances), and to which sufficient portions for Vicars were assigned'.[48]

In October 1537, shortly before the Dissolution, the prior and convent leased to William Saunder and Thomas Saunder, for 40 years at an annual rent of £2, the Rectory of Merton, with a tenement and parcel of land on the west side of the parish church, with a barn and close called the parsonage barn, and all tithes, oblations, mortuaries, profits, commodities, and advantages to the Rectory relating or pertaining ... the Lessees to provide a fit priest to celebrate in the said parish church, and also wine, bread, wax candles, and all necessaries which by ancient law pertained to the said church, and all other burthens, ordinary and extraordinary, chargeable upon the Rector.[49]

This parsonage barn and close would be the plots on which the later vicarage was built *c.*1818, together with the lands on which the present parish hall now stands, and the adjoining Glebe Meadow. In 1844 the tithe apportionment identifies these as 'glebe', plot 69 being the 'house and garden' (i.e. the Vicarage) of a little over half an acre, and plot 70 'Church Meadow' at almost 3 acres (see tithe map extract below).

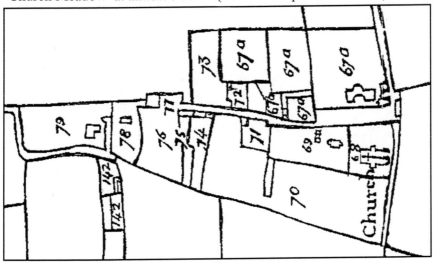

Plot 71 was a 'cottage and garden' belonging to James Sutton and occupied by George Groves, a copyhold property to which Sutton's father-in-law, William Head, had been admitted in 1806.[50] It was probably the 'cottage with yard called Telford in Church Streate' mentioned in the manorial court rolls between 1521 and 1627.[51]

The Locke family purchased the rectorial rights in 1552/3 and continued as lay rectors until 1644. They also owned the freehold property opposite the church, known in the 18th century as Merton Place and later as Church House. The rectorial rights were held by the owners of this property into the 19th century, and the barn that stood in the grounds of Church House was known as the tithe barn. However, the 1537 lease shows that the parsonage barn was then within the close opposite the Church House site, so the possibility exists that the pond was part of a moat that had protected the earlier tithe barn. The close would be that shown in the foreground of J Stratford's 1806 engraving of the south and west sides of St Mary's church, reproduced below.

It was probably this close that was granted by the priory to William de Cuteron in January 1310/11, described as

> that land in the ville of Merton which is called parroccheshawe, and is of the church land; to have and hold to himself and heirs, free from all secular exaction; he returning thence annually to the almoner 4s. sterling, and to find in autumn three men at a bederipe and one man for reaping, the almoner finding drink. William and his heirs to hold the land so long as they perform their part.[52]

It is likely that this area had been the original location of Merton priory which, when founded in 1114, occupied wooden buildings in the vicinity of the church that sheriff Gilbert had recently built and decorated at his own expense. However, the prior preferred the site by the Wandle, being attracted by its abundant water supply among its other benefits, and the community moved there in 1117.[53]

MORDEN HALL

The Morden Hall site is set among a complex system of channels and leats of the River Wandle, reflecting centuries of human adaptation of the river's course, as depicted on this extract from the 1st edition Ordnance Survey 25-inch map of 1864.

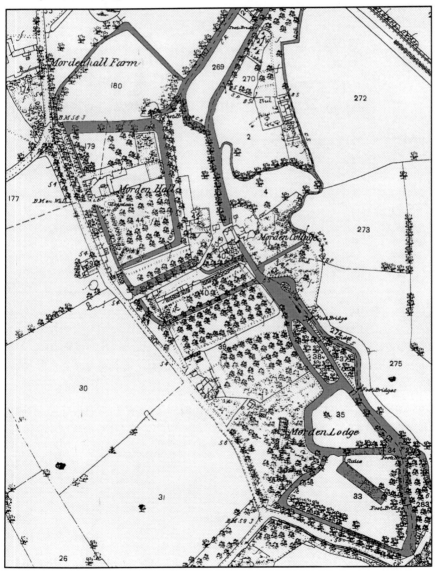

There is convincing documentary evidence, in the form of insurance policies, to show a building under construction in 1750 for the fifth Richard Garth, whose family had owned the manor of Morden since 1554. This was no doubt the present Morden Hall, now in the ownership of the National Trust, and depicted in this engraving published in Edward Walford's *Greater London* (1883).

In 1754 Richard married Mary Leheup, to whom were born three daughters who were to become coheiresses to the Morden estate. Following their marriages in 1774, 1775 and 1778, and the death of his wife in 1780, Richard Garth V moved to a house in west London, and the house was thereafter leased to tenants.[54]

But there had been an earlier 'mansion house' on the site. A list of leases dating from 1745, when Richard had come of age, begins with 'a capital messuage or mansion house with barns, stables, buildings, outhouses, dove houses and dove coat, yards, courtyards, gardens, orchards and premises' all leased, together with 34 acres of meadow and pasture land, to Peter and Stephen Mauvillain, proprietors of the calico printing works at nearby Ravensbury, and owners of a house adjoining the Morden Hall estate within the curtilage of the present Morden Lodge.[55] The lease had originated in 1716, and included use, liberty, priviledge and benefitt of cutting and digging trenches, ditches and drains as they can and lawfully may grant in any part of these above mentioned premises (except the yard, etc.) in order to bring such part of the River Wandle as they the said Peter and Stephen Mauvillain shall think necessary or convenient, in, by or through the said premises for the carrying on of the trade, profession, occupation or business of staining, dyeing, washing and printing of calicoes or such other stuffes, goods, wares, commodities, matters and things as now are or hereafter may or shall be used; And priviledge, use, right and interest in Fishery or priviledge of Fishing in the River Wandle ...[56]

Although many of the channels within the estate might have originated in such industrial uses, the house itself occupies a 5-acre site surrounded by water channels that have every indication of being a moat, though later adapted as a garden feature as portrayed in this illustration of c. 1790.[57]

This site had been occupied as the estate centre for centuries, and is identifiable as the 'capital messuage with a certain place within the court of which the easement of the cattle sheds are worth per annum 3s', in an extent or valuation of Westminster abbey's estate in Morden, made in 1312.[58] A 'Croft next to the Court' contained 1 acre of meadow worth 2s, as well as 2¾ acres of pasture, this distinction indicating riverside meadowland. This was likely to be the 'Croft' shown on a plan of 1859 (below) as occupying the area enclosed by a loop of the Wandle, and cut by the leat operating the 18th-century snuff mills which adjoin Morden Cottage.[59] The medieval mill was not valued in the 1312 extent as it was in the process of being rebuilt,[60] and was therefore not contributing to the manorial economy at that moment.

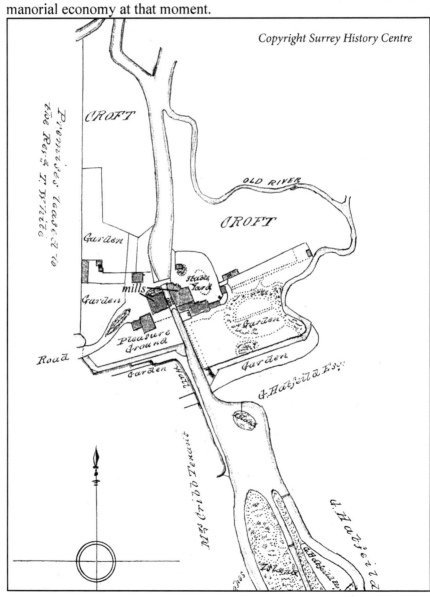

An agreement of November 1225 between the abbot and convent of Westminster, the prior and convent of nearby Merton, and Sir William de Mara who held the neighbouring manor later known as Ravensbury, probably indicates the date that the moat was created.[61] It records that

> the said abbot and convent of Westminster have granted to E the prior and convent of Merton and the lord W de Mara and his heirs in perpetuity, a common way for all riders and pedestrians and for carts direct from the northern and western corner of their court of Morden to the southern corner of their tenement in the same vill next to the house of William son of Sweyn on the west side, extending just as straight and best as possible, behind their court of Morden, going across their meadow that is there to the least harm, not only to the said abbot and convent of Westminster, but also to the prior and convent of Merton and W de Mara and his heirs, having in its breadth twelve feet, if the said abbot and convent, on both sides, wish it to be ditched, or if indeed they do not wish it to be ditched, by breadth of ten feet. Thus for this covenant and concession, the said prior and convent of Merton and W de Mara have resigned and quitclaimed to the abbot and convent of Westminster the road that they required from them going across their court of Morden and the pathway going across their meadow. Yet the said prior and convent of Merton and W de Mara, by reason of the same way and path that is required of them, henceforth are able to require from them another way.

The new road would be the present Morden Hall Road, and William son of Sweyn's house in the vicinity of the present Morden Lodge. The re-routing of a road that had previously crossed the abbot's court at Morden would be a necessary preliminary to the creation of a moat. And 1225 was also a key date in Westminster abbey's history, for it was the year in which the abbot allocated several manors, including Morden, to the support of the convent, reserving others to fund his own expenses.[62] A custumal of around this date reveals that the abbey was now managing all its estates directly through its own local managers, rather than leasing them to tenants, as had been its custom since the 11th century.[63] Morden itself was already leased 'at farm' in 1086, as Domesday Book records its value as 'now £10 and yet it renders £15'.[64] Now that the manorial centre was no longer occupied by a resident lessee, but managed by a local reeve who lived on his own customary tenement, it would seem that additional protection for the estate's crops and livestock, such as would be provided by a moat, was considered necessary.

27

RAVENSBURY

Although there was some inconsistency over the grid reference for this site, the description applies to plot 285 on this extract from the 1864/7 Ordnance Survey 25-inch maps, the channels enclosing about one acre.

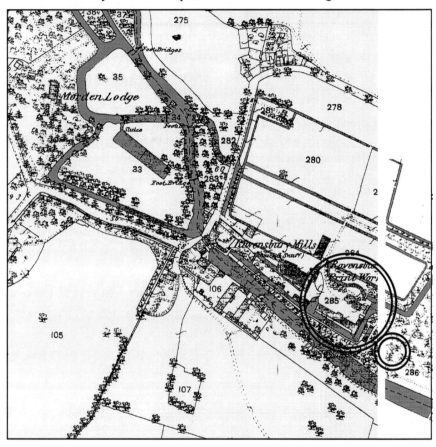

The late 17th- or early 18th-century Ravensbury Manor House, depicted in an 1825 watercolour by Yates (on facing page),[65] had occupied the riverside site to the east of this feature (marked by the smaller circle). This was probably on the site, or within the curtilage, of the 'capital messuage of the manor' first noted in extant records in an *inquisition post mortem* of 1313.[66] Is plot 285 another example of a moated enclosure for ancillary buildings adjoining the site of the house, as suggested above for Merton Place?

Another possibility is that this water feature was associated with the snuff mills adjoining the road, which first appear in extant records in a rental *c.*1680, when they were described as 'the new erected mill below Ravensbury'.[67] Previously 'Ravisbury mill' had referred to the 'millhouse and three water corn mills therein' above Mitcham bridge on the site of the Grove mill (see page 35),[68] but these had been lost to Reigate manor around 1590 after decades of legal wrangling.[69]

If not medieval, then a connection with the print works seems more likely, as its buildings lay in and around the 'moated' site. The parallel channels to the north were for calico bleaching, and Peter Mauvillain who, as we saw in the previous section, leased the nearby Morden Hall site, was operating a calico printing works at Ravensbury by 1719.[70]

In his first list, Dennis Turner mentioned a possible medieval fish-pond immediately to the east of plot 285. An even larger rectangular pond to the west of the present road in an island site between Morden Lodge and the snuff mills – plot 33 on the Ordnance Survey map – was known as Little Steelhaws from the 16th to 19th centuries, perhaps from *stell* or *stiell,* Old English for a fish-pond (though occasionally it was rendered Stenehawes or Stevenhawes after a nearby property).[71] It was within Ravensbury manor until 1588, when it was purchased by Richard Garth I, lord of the manor of Morden.

THE CANONS

This 17th-century house takes its name from the Augustinian canons of Southwark priory, who held an estate in Mitcham from the 12th century until the Dissolution. Close to an early 16th-century dovehouse in the grounds is a pond – plot 182 on this extract from the 1895 Ordnance Survey map. This pond formerly comprised two adjacent ponds, probably stews for breeding and holding freshwater fish so prized by monastic communities. There is no other documentary or map evidence to support the suggestion that this had once formed part of a moat. The water channel shown on the map running eastwards into the pond presumably flows from an artesian well that first appeared in 1822, as commemorated by the obelisk at the corner of Cricket Green and Madeira Road, and so must be a late feature, probably dug as a convenient way of getting rid of the excess spring water.[72]

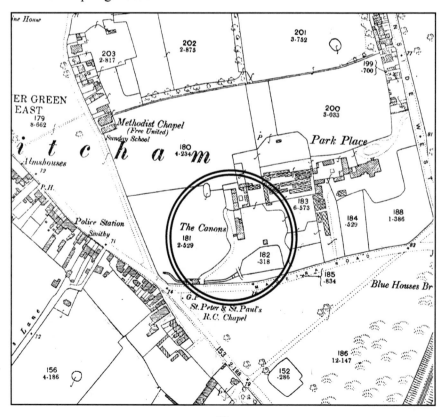

*Photographs, by E N Montague, of The Canons (above) in 1966,
the obelisk (below left) in 1975, and the dovehouse (below right) c.1970*

MITCHAM HALL

Among the earliest known benefactors of Southwark priory were members of the de Wicford family, whose many grants of land in Mitcham are recorded in the fragmentary remains of the priory's cartulary.[73]

There were two estates in Wicford or 'Whitford' recorded in Domesday Book, one held by William fitzAnsculf, the other by Odo, bishop of Bayeux, half-brother of William the Conqueror.[74]

Wicford takes its name from the ford across the Wandle, long superseded by Mitcham bridge, and the original 'wic' could well have been associated with the ancient 'oval enclosure' within the Morden section of Ravensbury manor (tithe plots 291, 310–322). FitzAnsculf's Wicford estate seems to have comprised that section of the later Ravensbury manor that lay within Morden, his estate in Mitcham closely matching the Mitcham section of Ravensbury.[75] After the death of the Conqueror, bishop Odo supported the king's eldest son Robert of Normandy against his younger brother William Rufus and, on the defeat of Robert, Odo's estates were confiscated. There is some evidence that his Wicford estate also came into the hands of fitzAnsculf, though it remained separate from the Ravensbury holdings, being held as a knight's fee of the fee of Barnack of the fitzAnsculf honor of Dudley.

The earliest mention of this knight's fee in the Mitcham area is from 1210–12 when, according to *The Red Book of the Exchequer,* Alexander de Wicford held half a knight's fee in Surrey of the honor of Dudley.[76] In 1242/43 an Alexander de Wycford is recorded as holding a full knight's fee in Mitcham of the honor of Dudley and the barony of Roger de Sumeri (a descendant of fitzAnsculf) during the reign of Henry III (not Henry I as stated by Lysons).[77] By 1428 the subsidy rolls recorded that John Burgh owed 6s 8d for 'one fee in Mitcham and Wandsworth, which William de Mareys had formerly held of the fee of Barnack',[78] so the former de Wicford estate had passed into the possession of William Mareys.

This was presumably the William Mareys who in 1361 granted, for a £5 annuity, an extensive though undefined estate in 'Wykeford in the parish of Mitcham' to the vicars of Mitcham and Morden, possibly in trust for Merton priory.[79] It is described as all my capital messuage with the buildings built upon it, gardens, crofts, meadows, pastures, woods, trees, fences, hedges, ditches just as it encloses [*sicut includit*], with two watermills and a certain piece of marshland [*more*] adjoining just as the water encloses it [*sicut aqua includit*] towards the field called Beneytesfeld and with all other their appurtenances which I have in Wykeford in the parish of Mitcham.

Later records indicate that Bennetsfield is the 23 acres in Morden within the loop of the Wandle south and east of Mitcham Bridge, now occupied by the National Trust's Watermeads and The Hub sports ground (see map on page 35).[80]

In January 1348/9 Mareys incurred a debt of £100 to Henry le Strete, a London vintner who had purchased the neighbouring 'Rasebury' estate in January 1346/7 and a further 60 acres from Mareys in the following October.[81] In February 1348/9 Mareys granted Strete a 25-year lease of his lands and tenements in Mitcham, Wicford, Wandsworth and Carshalton, enabling Strete to take the profits of the estate to recoup his losses – an arrangement on which he apparently reneged in 1361 when he granted an estate in trust to the vicars in return for an annuity.[82] Mareys had still not repaid his debt by September 1362, which seems to have brought Strete to ruin – a debt of £186 incurred by Strete in 1357, and still outstanding 15 years later after Strete's death, was bought up by the prior of Merton in 1373, the prior thereby acquiring a further interest in Mareys's estate, while the manor of Ravensbury was sold.[83] The priory was said to be holding 'the manor of Wykford' in 1380,[84] and at the Dissolution held lands in the vicinity of Mitcham Bridge as part of its Maresland or Mareshlandes estate 'in Mitcham and Carshalton'.[85] The lands can be traced through later documents, where they are described as 'Mareslondes', 'Marrish lands', 'Marris Fee' or 'Marsh Fee' lands.[86]

This disintegration of Mareys's estate is reflected in a 1402 assessment, made to levy an aid towards the marriage of Henry IV's daughter, which reveals that at that time William Mareys's knight's fee obligation had been divided among the prior of Merton, John Werbeltone, John Dymmok and John Grevyle who, through his wife, had inherited the manor of Ravensbury in 1391, no doubt including the 60 acres that Strete had purchased from Mareys in 1347.[87]

Was it Mareys's capital messuage that was enclosed by fences, hedges and ditches, or is this describing all his various landholdings? Could it be the former moated home of the de Wicford family? Eric Montague has suggested that this house may have stood on the site of the later Mitcham Hall, where 'there survived until the 1920s an L-shaped lake with the appearance of having formed part of a rectangular moat'.[88] It is likely to have been the 'great messuage' which James Wilford, a former alderman of the City of London and Master of the Worshipful Company of Merchant Taylors, bequeathed to his eldest son Robert in 1525. This bequest excluded two tenements on which his younger sons had already built houses, which can be identified with some confidence on the 1895 Ordnance Survey map as the site of the later so-called Manor House to the north of Mitcham Hall and a plot to the south on which had stood 'a little property' which played host to Elizabeth I on three occasions.[89]

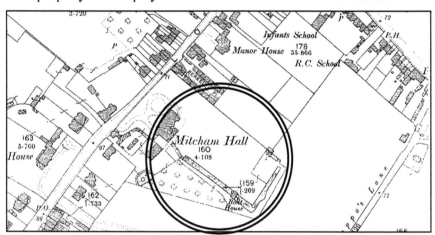

Robert Wilford certainly held the former priory estate called 'Mareslondes otherwise called Mareshfee with appurtenances in Mycham and Carsalton', but he obtained these, and other priory estates, by grant of the king in 1544, not by inheritance from his father.[90] It is possible that the de Wicford family home had been repurchased when the rest of their knight's fee holding was sold, as Mareys's father sold a house and 17 acres in Mitcham to Arnold de Wykeford at the end of the 13th century.[91]

A more likely location for William Mareys's capital messuage was on the Mitcham Grove site, discussed in the next section.

MITCHAM GROVE

In 1584, during a dispute over the mills above Mitcham bridge, reference was made to a 'messuage, two mills and 30 acres of land in Mitcham called the marrys', and the name Marris Fee or Marsh Fee is given to several other closes in Mitcham and Carshalton to the east of Mitcham bridge, indicating that they are likely to have formed part of Merton priory's Maresland or Mareshlandes estate in those two parishes.[92] These are identified by three dotted outlines added to this extract from the *Plan of Estates situate in the Parishes of Mitcham, Carshalton, Morden & Sutton in the County of Surrey* which accompanied the particulars of sale of the estate of Henry Hoare in 1828.[93]

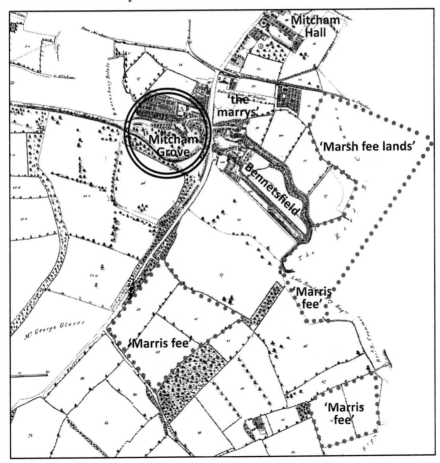

It is possible that other fields in this area had also been part of the priory's estate, though field name evidence has not survived.

Henry Hoare had held an extensive estate based on his home at Mitcham Grove, situated on an island between channels of the Wandle. Excavations conducted in 1974–5 revealed foundations and pottery from a 12th- or 13th-century building, its Tudor successor and Hoare's house built in the 18th century.[94]

The Tudor estate had been created from a variety of sources, including copyholds of Ravensbury and Vauxhall manors, the freehold mills and lands of Reigate manor, and freehold houses and lands purchased from several owners, not just the heirs of Robert Wilford. Thus we cannot be certain that the later Mitcham Grove had been within Merton priory's estate though, as Bennetsfield is just across the road from Mitcham Grove, and, as the site is enclosed by water, it is a firm contender for being the site of William Mareys's capital messuage mentioned in 1361.

However, the 1867 Ordnance Survey map (below) shows the irregular course of the streams that encompass the 5½-acre site of the former house demolished in 1845 – plot 288. As it shows none of the features we would expect of a medieval moat, if this is the site of Mareys's capital messuage, it is unlikely that any ditches that might have enclosed it in 1361 had formed a moat.

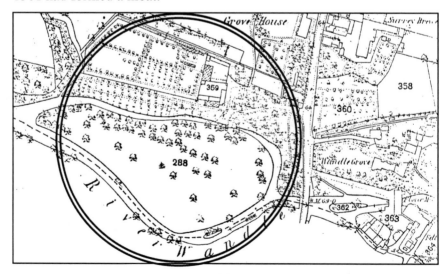

COLLIERS WOOD HOUSE

In this extract from the Ordnance Survey map of 1888, a long straight pond is shown at the rear of 'Manor House', formerly Colliers Wood House, its surrounding estate having been redeveloped for housing.

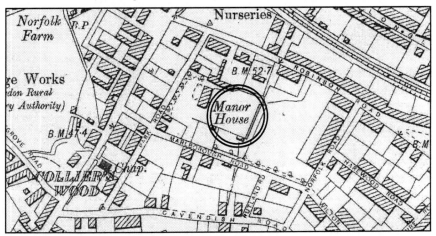

The Ordnance Survey map of 1867 seems to depict it as shrubbery.

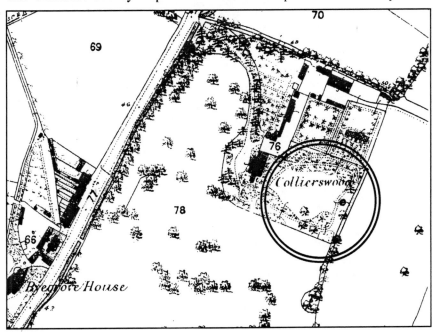

Similarly an estate map of 1824 does not indicate that this is a water feature, though it parallels the River Graveney, shown fronting the main road along the western boundary.[95]

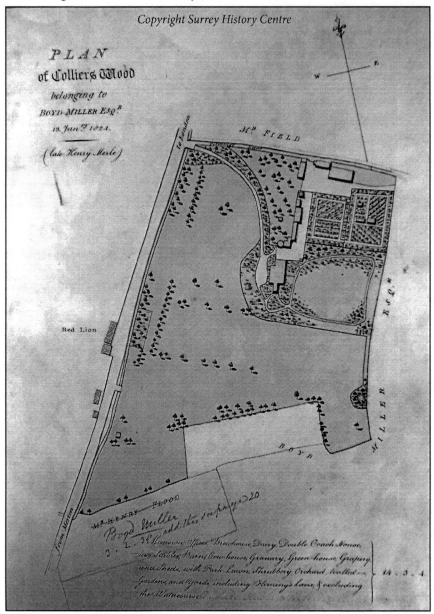

PLAN
of Colliers Wood
belonging to
BOYD MILLER ESQ.ʳ
13. Jan.ʸ 1824.
(late Henry Merle)

Red Lion

The river is presumably the 'shewer againste his close called Colliers Close lienge by the highe waye which leadithe from Marten abbaye to tootinge warde' that the then copyholder was instructed to cleanse in 1576, his neighbour being responsible for the next length as far as 'the brickbridge',[96] perhaps that named as 'Terriers Wood Bridge' over the Graveney on John Rocque's *Map of Ten Miles around London* of 1741–5. This shows the property of 'Peter de St Loy' – in fact Peter St Eloy, who was admitted to the copyhold in July 1739 – with ornamental canals meeting in a small round pond or 'basin'.[97] Could the 1888 pond, if such it is, be a remnant of this water feature?

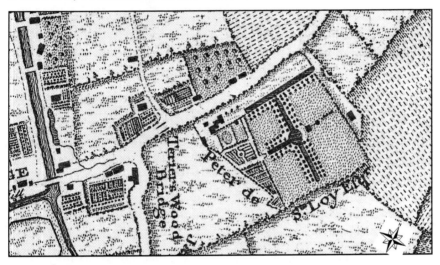

Eric Montague suggested that these 'straight lengths of water [were] possibly vestiges of a moated enclosure created in the Middle Ages, an hypothesis to which added credence is given by the house being situated on a spur of slightly elevated ground, defined by the 50-foot contour'.[98] He also notes that the old Mitcham–Tooting parish boundary, west of the present Colliers Wood High Street, 'followed a serpentine course across fields and through hedges', concluding that 'it perpetuated an ancient channel of the Graveney'.[99] He suggests that the river might have been diverted 'during the Middle Ages, perhaps with the intention of creating a partially moated enclosure for the homestead of Jenkingranger which then occupied the site of Colliers Wood House'. This name appears in the earliest extant court rolls of the manor of Ravensbury from 1487.[100]

CONCLUSIONS

This study has examined documentary evidence alongside that revealed on old maps, and together they seem to confirm the three sites within Dennis Turner's category of 'Certain and Probable Sites', to which can be added Merton Grange and Mitcham Hall.

The evidence suggests that **Merton Place**, formerly known as Moat House Farm, was on the site of the moated dovehouse belonging to Merton priory, and might even have incorporated part of its structure. Two arms survived into the 1820s. It was likely to have been a secondary moat, the primary moat having enclosed the adjoining **Merton Grange**.

At the priory's other farm, **West Barnes**, two arms of the moat survived into the 1930s, the house being called Moat Farm into the 19th century.

Similarly at **Mitcham Hall** two arms of the moat which had surrounded James Wilford's 'great messuage', probably on the site of the de Wicford family's medieval home, survived into the 1920s.

The only local moated site to survive today is at **Morden Hall**, probably dating from around 1225 when occupied as the manorial centre for Westminster abbey's estate in Morden. However, over the centuries additional channels have been dug, many of industrial origin to support the local calico bleaching and printing industries, though all have since been improved for aesthetic purposes.

Of Dennis Turner's 'Doubtful' moated sites, that at **Ravensbury** could possibly be associated with the medieval manorial centre nearby, though there is no documentary evidence for it. An industrial origin seems more likely, again probably associated with calico bleaching and printing.

Although the other sites have early water features, there is no evidence that any of them related to a moat. The pond near **St Mary's Church** may well have originated in the earliest period of Merton priory's occupation of this site, and it certainly predated the vicarage garden that finally engulfed it, but its precise purpose and form remain unknown.

The fishponds at **The Canons** are also medieval in origin, but again there is no evidence for a moat, the water channel feeding into the ponds post-dating the 1822 appearance of the artesian well.

Colliers Wood House certainly had extensive water features by the early 18th century and had been fronted by the re-routed River Graveney by the late 16th century, but there is no evidence that these were part of a moat surrounding the medieval house.

Although **Mitcham Grove** probably occupied the site of William Mareys's 'capital messuage' and has been surrounded by water since at least the 14th century, these watercourses are unlikely to have ever formed a formal moat.

All the sites considered above were of high status, most of them belonging to important medieval monastic establishments and manorial centres. Even Colliers Wood, though a copyhold property, became the centre for a substantial estate.

However, it must be remembered that ditches frequently enclosed even the humblest cottage, as this extract from the Morden manorial court roll for May 1389 reveals:

> At this court comes Ralph atte Rithe and surrenders into the lord's hand, for himself and his heirs forever, one cottage with curtilage adjoining, parcel of his tenement which he holds of the lord by roll of court, namely on the east of his tenement aforesaid as enclosed with hedge and ditch [*prout sep' & foss includit*]. And later the lord in open court grants the said cottage with appurtenances to William Pynnore and Lucy his wife, daughter of the aforesaid Ralph, to hold to themselves and theirs at the will of the lord in bondage by roll of court, by service, saving [the lord's] rights etc. And they give the lord for fine for entry as appears. And they do fealty.[101]

Ralph held a customary half-virgate tenement (about ten acres) fronting the green in Lower Morden Lane. This cottage was clearly built within the curtilage of his messuage plot, yet was enclosed by hedge and ditch to separate it from its parent holding.

It is likely that all the messuage plots here were similarly enclosed. It is certain that ditches ran along the roadside, as tenants were continually being ordered to scour them, under penalty of an amercement. Morden lies on the heavy London Clay, and ditches were essential for drainage. None of the other sites in this study were on the clay.

REFERENCES

1   *Surrey Archaeological Collections* 66 (1969) pp.113–4
2   *Surrey Archaeological Collections* 71 (1977) pp.89–94
3   Lambeth Archives Minet Deed 3764 (transcribed by John Wallace)
4   Surrey History Centre (SHC) 7883/5: abstract of title
5   London Metropolitan Archives (LMA), Guildhall Library Q2.8674/81 (13), p.207:
    Sun Insurance Policy 74383 (transcribed by John Wallace)
6   SHC 7883/5: abstract of title
7   SHC 7883/5: abstract of title
8   Quoted in Jack Russell *Nelson and the Hamiltons* (1969) pp.227–8
9   Engraving, in the author's possession, of '*Lord Nelson's Villa at Merton, Engraved
    by Amb. Warren from a Drawing by Gyford For Dr. Hughson's Description of
    London, Published by J. Stratford, 112, Holborn Hill March 1, 1806.*'
10 Merton Heritage & Local Studies Centre MerMor_Houses_Buildings_Merton_
    Place_16-6
11 The National Archives (TNA) SC 6/HenVIII/3463 m.5v
12 Janette Henderson *In Search of Merton Priory's Granges* (Merton Historical
    Society 2014) p.11
13 SHC 7883/3: abstract of title; Peter Hopkins *A History of Lord Nelson's Merton
    Place* (Merton Historical Society 1998)
14 Quotation from Fairburn's edition of *The Life of Admiral Lord Nelson* (Twenty-
    fifth edition) p.55. The original will was then in Somerset House, and a duplicate
    in the National Maritime Museum, Greenwich.
15 Peter Hopkins *Local History Notes 12: The Parish of Merton in 1844: The Tithe
    Apportionment Map* (Merton Historical Society 1998)
16 TNA SC 6/HenVIII/3463 m.5v
17 British Library (BL) Crach 1. Tab.1.b.1
18 Judith Goodman *Coal and Calico: Letters and Papers of the Bennett and Leach
    Families of Merton and Wandsworth* (Merton Historical Society 2008) p.183
19 Merton Parish Register, unpublished transcript by Stephen Turner of Merton
    Historical Society
20 Janette Henderson *In Search of Merton Priory's Granges* (Merton Historical
    Society 2014) p.11
21 Patent Rolls 7 Ed. VI, pt. xi, m. 25: *Calendar of Patent Rolls Edward VI 1547–
    1553* 5 (1926) pp.242–3
22 Patent Rolls 6 Eliz. pt. vi, m.18: TNA C 66/1001
23 SHC K85/3/28 p.32v
24 TNA A 4/15 f.151v
25 TNA 367/1030
26 TNA A 4/7 f.313v
27 TNA A 4/8 f.271
28 TNA A 4/9 f.69
29 TNA A 4/9 ff.176v, 178, 197
30 TNA A 4/11 f.312
31 TNA A 4/11 f.311v

32 TNA A 4/11 f.181v
33 TNA A 4/14 f.113
34 TNA A 4/17 f.41
35 TNA A 4/18 ff.169–169v
36 SHC G85/2/1/1/42 (transcribed by John Wallace)
37 Merton Heritage & Local Studies Centre MerMor_Houses_Buildings_Merton_ Place_16-3
38 LMA, Guildhall Library ms 34,100/205 roll 1 m.21
39 TNA SC 6/HenVIII/3463 m.6
40 Peter Hopkins *Discovering the Past 2: West Barnes & Cannon Hill* (2000)
41 TNA C 66/768 mm.11–12 (transcribed by John Wallace)
42 TNA C 66/1041 mm.28–9 (transcribed by John Wallace); SHC K212/71/2–5 (transcribed by John Wallace); TNA A 4/6 f.138v
43 TNA A 4/1 f.133
44 'West Barnes Farm, Now demolished: From a water-colour drawing in the possession of Mrs Lavender.' reproduced in W H Chamberlain *Reminiscences of Old Merton* (1925) p.54
45 O Manning & W Bray *The History and Antiquities of the County of Surrey* III (1814) p.cli
46 E M Jowett *Raynes Park: A Social History* (Merton Historical Society 1987) p.65
47 Janette Henderson *In Search of Merton Priory's Granges* (Merton Historical Society 2014) p.15
48 BL Cotton MS Cleopatra C. vii ff. cciiij–ccv.^{v} (no.548): A Heales *The Records of Merton Priory* (1898) pp.243–4
49 TNA SC 6/HenVIII/3463 m.6: translation A Heales *The Records of Merton Priory* (1898) p.344
50 John Innes Foundation Historical Collections TD 1513/4: Merton manorial court rolls: entry for 4.3.1806 (transcribed by John Wallace)
51 LMA Guildhall Library ms 34,100/205 roll 2 mm.9, 14, roll 4 mm.1, 2, 3v, 5, 11v
52 BL Cotton MS Cleopatra C. vii f.clix.^{v} (no.373): A Heales *The Records of Merton Priory* (1898) p.204
53 College of Arms Arundel MS 28 ff.1–3: M L Colker 'Latin Texts concerning Gilbert, founder of Merton Priory' in *Studia Monastica* 12 (1970) pp.248–249. A translation of this important document has been commissioned by Merton Historical Society.
54 W J Rudd *Morden Hall* (Merton Historical Society 1998) p.4
55 SHC K85/2/51–52
56 SHC 683/1
57 Judith Goodman *Merton & Morden: A Pictorial History* (Phillimore 1995) illustration 8, reproduced in the present publication courtesy of Sotheby's
58 Cambridge University Library Kk 5.29 39v–43v: images and translation available at http://www.mertonhistoricalsociety.org.uk/index.php?cat=projects&sec=!extent1312
59 SHC K85/2/353
60 Westminster Abbey Muniments (WAM) 27304; WAM 9289 m.1; Society of Antiquaries London MS 555 m.1

61 WAM 'Westminster Domesday' 169b–170a; BL Cotton MS Cleopatra C. vii f.cxj.^{v} (no.194)
62 Barbara Harvey *Westminster Abbey and its Estates in the Middle Ages* (1977) p.78
63 WAM 9287; BL Add Ch 8139
64 Domesday Book f.32r, 6: Ann Williams and G H Martin *Domesday Book: A Complete Translation* (Penguin 2002) p.77
65 'Mitcham – Ravensbury Manor House – Mrs Barnard': a rear view in a watercolour by Yates dated 1825, in an extra-illustrated copy of E W Brayley *History of Surrey* (Vol. III), by courtesy of Merton Library & Heritage Service Mit_Buildings_32-1
66 TNA C 134/32 (18) m.3: *Calendar of Inquisitions Post Mortem* 5 (1908) 445 p.250
67 SHC 212/9/2 m.3; E N Montague *Mitcham Histories 10: Ravensbury* (Merton Historical Society 2008) p.83
68 SHC 320/1/13 p.8; 303/21/4/1–4
69 TNA C 2/Eliz/H17/3; see also SHC 643/2/3; SHC 371/2/5/1&2 = SHC 3537/1/21 (p.50 entry 63) =3537/1/22 (p.31 entry 63); 371/2/5/4 = 3537/1/23 (p.23); TNA CP 25/2/228/37&38ELIZIMICH; SHC 3537/1/23 (p.23) = 371/2/5/4; TNA STAC 3/6 (25), 3/8 (2), 4/2 (65), 4/4 (12); BL Add Ch 23560; BL Add Roll 23557
70 E N Montague *Mitcham Histories 10: Ravensbury* (Merton Historical Society 2008) p.63
71 BL Add Ch 23643 8r, 9r; Add Ch 23644 3r, 1v; Add Ch 23646 1r; SHC K85/2/12; K85/2/18; K85/3/28 pp.18–20; 320/1/13 p.65; TNA C 66/1309 m.14; TNA A 4/4 f.231v; Peter Hopkins *Local History Notes 13: Morden in 1838: The Tithe Apportionment Map* (Merton Historical Society 1998) plot 353; A H Smith *English Place-Name Elements* II (1956) p.150
72 E N Montague *Mitcham Histories 11: The Cranmers, The Canons and Park Place* (Merton Historical Society 2011) pp.73–105
73 BL Add MS 6040 f.1 nos. 1 & 2, f.2 no. 20: translation by Dr R A M Scott from a transcript by Dr J Blair; E N Montague *Mitcham Histories 11: The Cranmers, The Canons and Park Place* (Merton Historical Society 2011) pp.11–13
74 Domesday Book ff.31v, 5 & 35v, 21: A Williams & G H Martin (ed) *Domesday Book: A Complete Translation* (Penguin 2001) pp.75, 84
75 Peter Hopkins *Medieval Morden: Landscape and Landholding* (in preparation)
76 TNA E 164/2 f.146v (249v): H Hall (ed) *The Red Book of the Exchequer* (1896) p.560
77 *Liber Feodorum: The Book of Fees commonly called Testa de Nevill II: AD 1242–1292* (1923) p.687; O Manning & W Bray *The History and Antiquities of the County of Surrey* II (1809) p.499; D Lysons *The Environs of London I: Surrey* (1792) p.351 citing BL Harl MS 313 f.15, but the entries on this folio are from the reign of Henry III according to *A Catalogue of the Harleian Manuscripts in the British Museum* I (1808) p.194. The de Sumery connection was through the first marriage of Gervase Paynell's daughter, long after the time of Henry I.
78 TNA E 179/184/75 rot.3 mm.2–3: Subsidy Rolls 1428: Surrey: Wallington Hundred, transcribed in *Inquisitions and Assessments relating to Feudal Aids 1284–1431* V (1908) p.124

79 TNA C 54/199 m.3d: Close Roll 35 Edward III (1361–1362): *Calendar of Close Rolls Edward III 11 1360–1364* (1909) p.302

80 BL Add Ch 23637 8r, 10r

81 TNA C 241/143 (64); TNA CP 25/1/229/49 no.9: Feet of Fines Surrey 21 Edw III; TNA CP 25/1/229/49 no.12: Feet of Fines Surrey 21 Edw III

82 TNA E 40/5695

83 TNA C 241/143 (64); C 131/190/33 m.1, 1v; C 131/20 (23) m.1, 1v, 2; C 131/20 (14) m.1; C 131/20 (15) m.2 (the extent for C 131/20 (14) was attached to C 131/20 (15) and vice versa); TNA C 54/211 m.34d: *Calendar of Close Rolls* XIII (1911) p.544: Close Rolls 47 Ed III m.34d; TNA CP 25/1/230/60 no.4: Feet of Fines Surrey 1 Ric II

84 TNA C 143/395/28

85 *Valor Ecclesiasticus* (1814) ii 48; TNA SC 6/HENVIII/3463 m.11

86 SHC 77/4/1; 212/113/18a; 230/1; 230/2; 599/219 a–b; 599/221; 599/390 a–d; 599/391 a–d

87 *Inquisitions and Assessments relating to Feudal Aids 1284–1431* VI (1920) p.389

88 E N Montague *Mitcham Histories 4: Lower Mitcham* (Merton Historical Society 2003) pp.5, 9

89 E N Montague *Mitcham Histories 4: Lower Mitcham* (Merton Historical Society 2003) pp.15–18

90 SHC 599/219 a–b: 3 copies of a translation of a grant in fee-farm of the manors of Biggin and Tamworth and other lands in Mitcham, late Merton Priory, 19.5.1544=Pat Roll 36 Hen VIII pt.27 m.22 (29)

91 TNA E 40/9189, dated by Dr John Blair in a letter to E N Montague

92 TNA C 2/Eliz/H17/3; SHC 77/4/1; 212/113/18a; 230/1–2; 470/1 p.5

93 London Borough of Sutton Archives 2361/2/2; Croydon Library HW904

94 D G Bird 'Excavations at Mitcham Grove, 1974–5' in E N Montague *Mitcham Histories 10: Ravensbury* (Merton Historical Society 2008) pp.175–8

95 SHC 320/2/1 p.3

96 G L Gomme *Court Minutes of the Surrey and Kent Sewer Commission 1569–1570* I (London County Council 1909) 973–4, p.252

97 E N Montague *Mitcham Histories 9: Colliers Wood or 'Merton Singlegate'* (Merton Historical Society 2007) pp.52–4

98 E N Montague *Mitcham Histories 9: Colliers Wood or 'Merton Singlegate'* (Merton Historical Society 2007) p.46

99 E N Montague *Mitcham Histories 9: Colliers Wood or 'Merton Singlegate'* (Merton Historical Society 2007) p.22

100 SHC 320/1/13 pp.52–55; BL Add Ch 23548 2r

101 BL Add Roll 56039 3r

FURTHER READING FROM

Judith Goodman *Coal and Calico: Letters and Papers of the Bennett and Leach Families of Merton and Wandsworth* (2008)

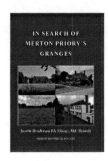

Janette Henderson *In Search of Merton Priory's Granges* (2014)

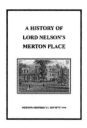

Peter Hopkins *Local History Notes 12: The Parish of Merton in 1844: The Tithe Apportionment Map* (1998)

Peter Hopkins *Local History Notes 13: Morden in 1838: The Tithe Apportionment Map* (1998)

Peter Hopkins *A History of Lord Nelson's Merton Place* (1998)

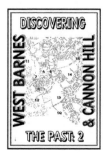

Peter Hopkins *Discovering the Past 2: West Barnes & Cannon Hill* (2000)